Oceans and Seas of the World Homeschool Geography 3rd Grade Series

A sea is smaller than
an ocean. The sea is a
part of the ocean that is
partially enclosed by land.

OCEANS

An ocean is a large body
of saline water that
composes much of the
planet's hydrosphere.

The largest bodies of water on Earth are the Pacific Ocean, Atlantic Ocean, Indian Ocean, Southern Ocean, and Arctic Ocean.

The largest
ocean on Earth
is the Pacific
Ocean, it covers
around 30%
of the Earth's
surface. The
Pacific Ocean
contains around
25000 different
islands.

The second largest ocean on Earth is the Atlantic Ocean, it covers over 21% of the Earth's surface.

SEAS

A sea is a large body of salt water that is surrounded in whole or in part by land.

Seas only
partially
landlocked
and bounded
by submarine
ridges on
the sea floor
are often
referred too as
marginal seas.

The sea moderates the Earth's climate and has important roles in the water cycle, carbon cycle, and nitrogen cycle.

The Mediterranean Sea s a sea connected to the Atlantic Ocean surrounded by the Mediterranean region and almost completely enclosed by land.